NATIVE PEOPLES OF NORTH AMERICA

Native Peoples of THE GREAT PLAINS

By Lynda Arnéz

Gareth Stevens PUBLISHING

Please visit our website, www.garethstevens.com. For a free color catalog of all our high-quality books, call toll free 1-800-542-2595 or fax 1-877-542-2596.

Library of Congress Cataloging-in-Publication Data

Names: Arnéz, Lynda.
Title: Native peoples of the Great Plains / Lynda Arnéz.
Description: New York : Gareth Stevens Publishing, [2016] | Series: Native peoples of North America | Includes index.
Identifiers: LCCN 2015045647 | ISBN 9781482448252 (pbk.) | ISBN 9781482448115 (library bound) | ISBN 9781482447613 (6 pack)
Subjects: LCSH: Indians of North America–Great Plains–History–Juvenile literature.
Classification: LCC E78.G73 A76 2016 | DDC 978.004/97–dc23
LC record available at http://lccn.loc.gov/2015045647

First Edition

Published in 2017 by
Gareth Stevens Publishing
111 East 14th Street, Suite 349
New York, NY 10003

Copyright © 2017 Gareth Stevens Publishing

Designer: Samantha DeMartin
Editor: Kristen Nelson

Photo credits: Series art AlexTanya/Shutterstock.com; cover, p. 1 Stock Montage/Archive Photos/Getty Images; p. 5 (main) RRuntsch/Shutterstock.com; p. 5 (map) AlexCovarrubias/Wikimedia Commons; p. 7 Henry Guttmann/Hulton Archive/Getty Images; p. 9 Apic/Hulton Archive/Getty Images; p. 11 (main) Windmill Books/Universal Images Group/Getty Images; p. 11 (inset) Culture Club/Hulton Archive/Getty Images; p. 13 William Henry Jackson/Hulton Archive/Getty Images; p. 15 ullstein bild/ullstein bild/Getty Images; p. 17 Buyenlarge/Archive Photos/Getty Images; pp. 19, 21 Print Collector/Hulton Archive/Getty Images; p. 23 DEA PICTURE LIBRARY/De Agostini/Getty Images; p. 25 UniversalImagesGroup/Universal Images Group/Getty Images; p. 27 MPI/Archive Photos/Getty Images.

All rights reserved. No part of this book may be reproduced in any form without permission in writing from the publisher, except by a reviewer.

Printed in the United States of America

CPSIA compliance information: Batch #CS16GS: For further information contact Gareth Stevens, New York, New York at 1-800-542-2595.

CONTENTS

Great and Large 4
Constant Movement 6
Horses Arrive 8
The Hunt 10
Other Homes 12
In the Band 14
Men, Women, and Children 16
The Spiritual World 18
Disease 20
The US Grows West 22
The Comanche 24
The Cheyenne 26
Battling Together 28
Glossary 30
For More Information 31
Index 32

Words in the glossary appear in **bold** type the first time they are used in the text.

Great and LARGE

The Great Plains region, or area, in North America is around 1 million square miles (2.59 million sq km). It **stretches** from the Missouri and the Mississippi River valleys in the east to the Rocky Mountains in the west.

People have lived in this huge region for at least 10,500 years, and possibly much longer! The earliest people there were **ancestors** of the more than 30 groups that make up the native peoples of the Great Plains. Though each group had its own **culture**, the groups also shared many ways of life.

TELL ME MORE

The Great Plains is mostly flat. The weather is hot and dry in the south, wetter near the river valleys, and can be quite cold in the north during winter.

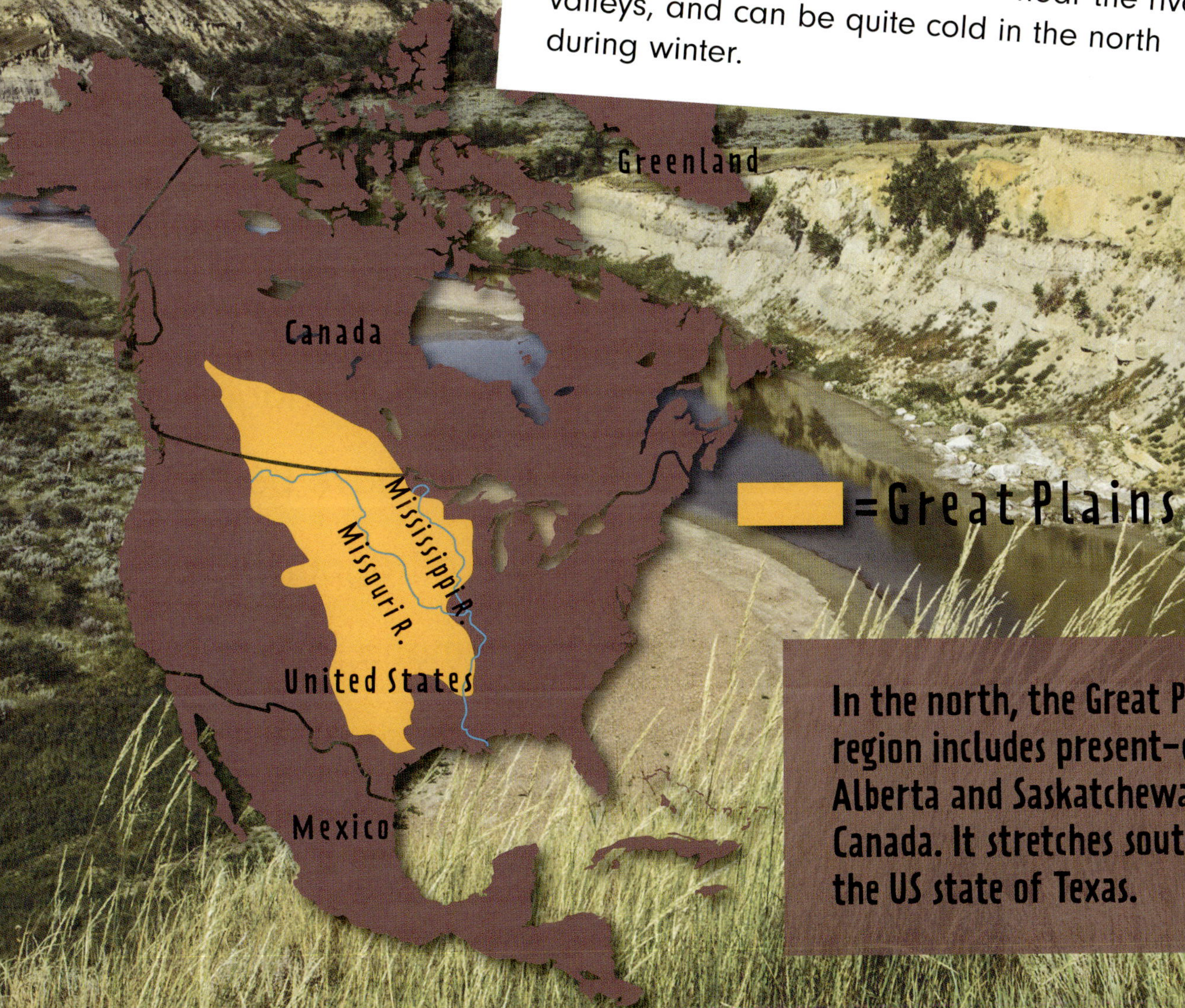

In the north, the Great Plains region includes present-day Alberta and Saskatchewan in Canada. It stretches south through the US state of Texas.

Constant MOVEMENT

For the most part, native peoples on the plains were **nomads** who hunted and gathered their food. They planned their lives around the movement of the buffalo, or bison. In the spring and summer, small groups would come together to hunt the bison as the animals gathered to have babies. In the winter, the small groups would split off again.

Some groups, such as the Hidatsa, Omaha, and Pawnee, set up **permanent** villages as early as AD 1100. These Plains Village cultures farmed as well as hunted.

Nomads on the plains built tepees, cone-shaped homes made of bison or animal hide and wooden poles. The tepees were light and easy to move.

TELL ME MORE

By the 1700s, native peoples from the North American Northeast were being forced west by European settlements. Many of them also came to live on the Great Plains.

Horses ARRIVE

Life for all native peoples of the Great Plains changed a lot during the mid-1500s. The Spanish began to explore North America around this time, and they brought horses with them. By about 1750, horses were common on the Great Plains.

Hunters riding horses could now keep up with herds of bison. It became easier to feed big groups of people. Before horses, trained dogs pulled **sleds** full of supplies. Now, native peoples could travel with more and move it more quickly.

TELL ME MORE

Horses had so much value that one native group would attack another just to steal them!

Horses so affected the lives of the Plains peoples that historians divide their history into "before" and "after" the introduction of horses.

The HUNT

Before encountering any Europeans, the native peoples of the Great Plains hunted on foot using bows and arrows. By the 1700s, fur traders introduced them to guns. At first, hunters didn't use guns because they weren't **accurate**. But as the guns got better, hunting using guns and horses became common.

Within the Plains Village cultures, there were seasons of hunting and farming. The Arikara, for example, planted in the spring, hunted bison through the summer, and returned to their village to **harvest** in the fall.

TELL ME MORE

Hunting bison was the main way Plains peoples fed and clothed their families.

Native groups that farmed on the Great Plains grew beans, squash, and corn. In addition, most groups gathered seeds, wild fruit, nuts, and roots.

Other HOMES

Native groups living in permanent villages built large homes called earth lodges. They had **domed** roofs and walls made of earth and were mostly circular inside. Three **generations** of one family often lived together in one earth lodge.

Another home commonly built by the Osage and Wichita peoples looked somewhat like a wickiup, a home often built in the Northeast. Wickiups were cone-shaped and made of bent poles and covered in either animal skins or grass.

Earth lodges were big enough for favorite dogs and horses to stay inside, too!

TELL ME MORE

The opening of earth lodges and tepees was commonly facing the rising sun.

In the BAND

Within the many cultural groups of native peoples on the Great Plains were communities called bands. They had their own leaders and often joined with other bands to hunt or travel together. A band could be fewer than 50 people or a few hundred!

How each band worked depended on the culture. The Skidi band of the Pawnee, for example, tried to be totally independent from the other Pawnee bands. On the other hand, people easily came and went from one Comanche (kuh-MAN-chee) band to another.

Many Plains peoples had societies within their band that took care of certain duties, such as one that would make sure everyone followed a leader's orders.

TELL ME MORE

The native peoples of the Great Plains are sometimes grouped together by language. However, this grouping overlooks the independent bands within these groups.

Men, Women, and CHILDREN

Both men and women had important jobs to do within the native communities on the Great Plains. Men hunted and took part in **defending** their band. Women took care of children, gathered plant foods, and cooked. They also built and cared for the home and made clothing.

On the plains, men and women commonly married only one person. However, women had a lot of work to do. Sometimes, a woman and her sister would have the same husband to share duties and care for the family better.

Some Plains peoples were patrilineal, meaning they traced family ties through a person's father. Others were matrilineal and traced family through a person's mother. Still others used both!

TELL ME MORE

Children learned to do their adult jobs as they played. Boys had toy bows and arrows, and girls were given dolls and taught to sew clothes for them.

The Spiritual WORLD

Nature played a big part in the spiritual lives of the native peoples of the Great Plains. They commonly believed that animals, the sun, plants, and other natural elements were the earthly **representations** of spirits.

Most native peoples on the Great Plains believed there were many spirits. Some, such as the Crow, believed all these spirits were equal in power. The Cheyenne believed in two more important gods, the "Wise One above" and one that lived underground.

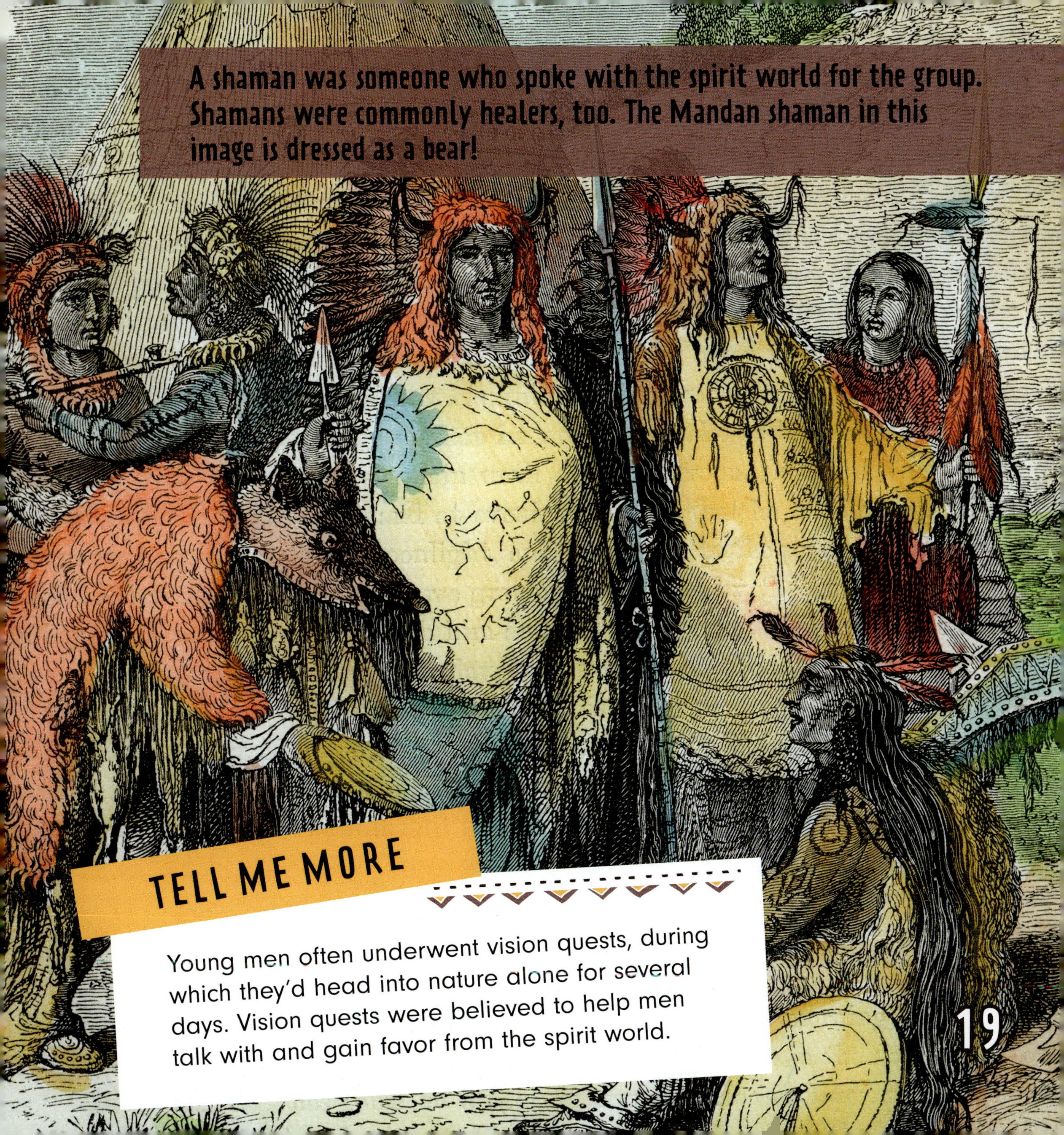

A shaman was someone who spoke with the spirit world for the group. Shamans were commonly healers, too. The Mandan shaman in this image is dressed as a bear!

TELL ME MORE

Young men often underwent vision quests, during which they'd head into nature alone for several days. Vision quests were believed to help men talk with and gain favor from the spirit world.

DISEASE

By the late 18th century, British fur traders had begun building trading posts on the Great Plains. Their trade didn't affect the Plains peoples as much as the introduction of Spanish horses. But the diseases, or illnesses, they brought with them did.

The native peoples' bodies had never encountered sicknesses such as smallpox and measles before. They couldn't fight them off, and many died. Those living in villages faced the most danger, as the illnesses spread quickly where people lived near each other.

The native peoples on the plains would trade furs and skins with the British and French for pots, knives, guns, and kettles.

TELL ME MORE

The children of European fathers and native mothers were called the Métis. They often grew up with a mixture of both cultures.

The US Grows WEST

During the 1840s, settlers from the United States began traveling west by wagon. Pathways across the plains, such as the Oregon Trail, passed through the lands of many Plains peoples. The wagon trains drove away the bison and destroyed big areas of grassland, harming native ways of life.

By the late 1800s, large groups of native peoples from all over North America were forced onto land set aside for them called reservations. Many people died fighting against reservations.

Some groups of native peoples on the Great Plains attacked settlers who tried to live on their land.

TELL ME MORE

The United States made and broke many treaties, or agreements, with the native groups living within the country. Some people believe these wrongs still need to be made up for today.

The COMANCHE

The Comanche lived in the area of present-day Wyoming and moved south on the Great Plains over time. They were one of the first groups to use horses and were known for their skill with them. The Comanche were some of the only native peoples who could fight on horseback.

By the early 1800s, the Comanche were one of the most powerful peoples living on the Great Plains. They were made up of about 13 bands with possibly up to 30,000 people total.

TELL ME MORE

"Comanche" is a Ute word that means "anyone who wants to fight me all the time."

Today, the Comanche Nation is found on a reservation in Lawton, Oklahoma.

The CHEYENNE

Though the Cheyenne became bison hunters like the other native peoples on the Great Plains, they were farmers first. Before 1700, they lived in present-day Minnesota where they farmed and made clay pots. They later moved to what's now North Dakota, where they began hunting bison on horseback. They moved around more during the 1800s, with a large group making their home on the Arkansas River.

The Cheyenne enjoyed celebrations and **ceremonies**. Leaders smoked a peace pipe before they met to discuss their people's needs and problems.

The Cheyenne joined other native groups of the Great Plains to fight the US government during the late 1800s.

TELL ME MORE

The 10 Cheyenne bands were led by 44 chiefs.

Battling TOGETHER

One of the most famous Native American heroes, Sitting Bull, was a Lakota chief on the Great Plains. He was a spiritual leader for the many Plains people who fought in the Battle of the Little Bighorn in 1876.

This was just one battle between US forces and those living on the Great Plains. The native peoples of the Great Plains won the battle, showing their bravery and loyalty to their people. Nonetheless, US forces successfully forced most Plains peoples onto reservations soon after.

Who are some native peoples of the Great Plains?

Mandan

Lakota

Shawnee

Dakota

Comanche

Hidatsa

Blackfoot

Lipan Apache

Osage

Arapaho

Nakota

Cheyenne

TELL ME MORE

The Lakota, Dakota, and Nakota are part of a big group called the Sioux that all spoke languages from the same family.

GLOSSARY

accurate: able to hit the target

ancestor: a family member who lived long before another

ceremony: an event to honor or celebrate something

culture: the beliefs and ways of life of a group of people

defend: to guard against harm

domed: having an arched and rounded shape

generation: a group of individuals born about the same time

harvest: to bring in a crop

nomad: someone who moves from place to place based on the seasons

permanent: something that won't change

representation: something that stands in place of

sled: a cart with runners that moves over ice and snow

stretch: to reach across

For More INFORMATION

Books

Bowman, Donna Janell. *The Sioux: The Past and Present of the Dakota, Lakota, and Nakota.* North Mankato, MN: Fact Finders, 2015.

Suen, Anastasia. *Great Plains Region.* Vero Beach, FL: Rourke Educational Media, 2015.

Yasuda, Anita. *Native Nations of the Plains.* Mankato, MN: Child's World, 2015.

Websites

American Indians – Plains Tribes & Southeastern Tribes
kidzworld.com/article/1303-american-indians-plains-tribes-and-southeastern-tribes
Find out more about how the peoples of the Great Plains lived.

Cheyenne Indian Fact Sheet
bigorrin.org/cheyenne_kids.htm
This website answers many questions about the Cheyenne people of the Great Plains.

Publisher's note to educators and parents: Our editors have carefully reviewed these websites to ensure that they are suitable for students. Many websites change frequently, however, and we cannot guarantee that a site's future contents will continue to meet our high standards of quality and educational value. Be advised that students should be closely supervised whenever they access the Internet.

INDEX

bands 14, 15, 16, 24, 27
Battle of the Little Bighorn 28
bison 6, 7, 8, 10, 11, 22, 26
Cheyenne 18, 26, 27, 29
Comanche 14, 24, 25, 29
Crow 18
culture 4, 14, 21
earth lodges 12, 13
farming 6, 10, 11, 26
guns 10, 21
Hidatsa 6, 29
horses 8, 9, 10, 13, 20, 24
illnesses 20
jobs 16, 17
Mandan 19, 29
Mississippi River valley 4
Missouri River valley 4
nomads 6, 7
Omaha 6
Osage 12, 29
Pawnee 6, 14
Plains Village culture 6, 10
reservations 22, 25, 28
settlers 22, 23
shaman 19
Sitting Bull 28
Spanish 8, 20
spirits 18, 19
tepees 7, 13
treaties 23
vision quests 19
Wichita 12
wickiup 12